On The Job
in a Restaurant

by Jessica Cohn

RED
CHAIR
·PRESS·

Please visit our website at **www.redchairpress.com** for more high-quality products for young readers.

Publisher's Cataloging-In-Publication Data

Cohn, Jessica.
   On the job in a restaurant / by Jessica Cohn.

   pages : illustrations ; cm. -- (On the job)

   Summary: "Do you like to eat different foods? Maybe you like to help in the kitchen by cooking or bringing food to the table. Running restaurants large and small is no easy task as you will discover when you go On the Job in a Restaurant."--Provided by publisher.

   Includes writing activity and first-person interview.
   Includes bibliographical references and index.
   ISBN: 978-1-63440-110-4 (library hardcover)
   ISBN: 978-1-63440-116-6 (paperback)
   ISBN: 978-1-937529-54-3 (ebook)

   1. Restaurants--Vocational guidance--Juvenile literature. 2. Cooking--Vocational guidance--Juvenile literature. 3. Waiters and waitresses--Juvenile literature. 4. Restaurants--Vocational guidance. 5. Cooking--Vocational guidance. 6. Waiters and waitresses. I. Title. II. Title: In a restaurant

TX945 .C64 2016
647.95023   2015953631

Illustration credits: p. 4, 8, 9, 12, 14, 15, 16, 19, 22, 25, 29, 30, 32: Lauren Scheuer

Photo credits: Cover, p. 9, 18, 19, 22-23, 24, 26 (left), 28-29: Shutterstock; p. 1, 3, 5, 7 (top left), 12-13, 14, 16-17, 17, 25, 26 (right), 27 (left, right): iStock; p. 4-5, 6, 7 (top right), 8: Dreamstime; p. 7 (bottom): Lena Kwak; p. 10-11: © Mark Scheuern/Alamy; p. 20, 21: Stephanie Secrest; p. 32: Nathan Cohn

This series first published by:
Red Chair Press LLC   PO Box 333   South Egremont, MA 01258-0333

Printed in the United States of America

Distributed in the U.S. by Lerner Publisher Services. www.lernerbooks.com

0516 1 WRZF16

Table of Contents

Jobs in Hospitality

The kitchen and dining areas are filled with activity, even before the doors open. Servers listen to details about the night's specials. The manager makes sure the tables are ready.

Opening a new restaurant is a big undertaking. You need to find a good location. The food has to be interesting and delicious. And it should be priced well. The place must look and feel welcoming.

"I've worked as a cook . . . a server . . . a manager," says Briana Fore. She runs a restaurant that just opened in Oregon. The first days were hard, she says. "I had all the knowledge of what it takes to open a place," she adds. "Still, it's challenging. So many little things need to be covered."

The restaurant business is not easy. But this **profession** can be rewarding. Adults in North America buy food or drinks from restaurants nearly five times each week on average. Feeding all of those people keeps plenty of workers busy.

Roman Empire
The empire was at its height in the year A.D. 117 or so. People traveled to marketplaces, which grew as the cities did. Inns opened along the roads, where the travelers could eat.

France after the Revolution Only the rich had chefs before the revolution, which ended in 1799. Then, the ruling class was overthrown. The chefs were free to bring fine dining to the masses.

Modern America
The first McDonald's opened in the 1940s. It offered low-priced food fast. In 1954 Ray Kroc bought the place. He turned the new fast-food concept into a chain of restaurants.

On the Menu

Restaurants are a large part of the North American **economy**. How large? Almost half of the money spent on food goes to restaurants. There are almost a million places to eat in the U.S. and Canada.

Keeping customers happy is part art and part science. Some dishes change with the seasons. For example, some places cook with apples during apple season. The people who run restaurants also follow trends. Teens and younger people care more about their health now. So more places are offering healthy kids' meals.

>> You Know It!

STEM stands for **Science, Technology, Engineering,** and **Math**. People in the restaurant industry use these studies to find new or better ways of preparing and serving meals.

Experiments with Food

Fine restaurants sometimes have labs. These are special kitchens where chefs try out new recipes. Lena Kwak is a California chef who invented a new flour while working at a lab. It took lots of trial and error on her part.

Kwak's job was to help people on special diets. She worked like a scientist to make flour with no gluten. That is a **protein** found in grains. It makes some people feel ill.

What tech trends stand out?

Technology is changing the business of eating out. In some places, people can place orders on computer tablets. Restaurants with take-out service are also trying out plates, spoons, and other items made from plants, such as corn and beets. These bioplastic items breakdown in the trash. They do not hurt the **environment**.

In Charge of the House

"Ninety percent of restaurant managers started as hourly paid employees—working their way up to management." Dawn Sweeney, president of the National Restaurant Association (U.S.)

A manager at an eatery has the same kinds of questions that shop owners do. How do the customers feel? Do the workers know how to act? How do we attract new customers? Are we making enough money? Can we save money?

A restaurant is a kind of **retail** business. It sells meals. But is also sells the experience of eating out. Workers look for ways to encourage customers to spend more money on each visit. Popular chains make more than 2 million dollars a year at each store.

Friendly Faces

Restaurants are often called "houses" by those in the business. The workers that the customers see are in the "front of the house." The people in the kitchen or elsewhere work in the "back."

Managers work in both areas. There may be one manager for the front and another for the back. There may be a general manager over them both. A place that holds special events has banquet managers. Businesses that **cater** events will have a manager for that. Most of them need skill with mathematics.

Point of POS

A point of sale (POS) system can help managers keep track of sales and more. Computers in a POS system keep track of

- sales,

- cash flow,

- food **inventory**,

- orders.

POS systems have the technology needed to take card payments from bank accounts.

9

Generally Speaking

Amy Grossi runs the Bavarian Inn in Frankenmuth. The inn is famous for its chicken dinners. "We're a destination restaurant," she says. The town of Frankenmuth is in Michigan. But it looks like a town in old Germany. It draws a lot of travelers. The inn serves 900,000 people each year.

Bavarian Inn, Frankenmuth, MI

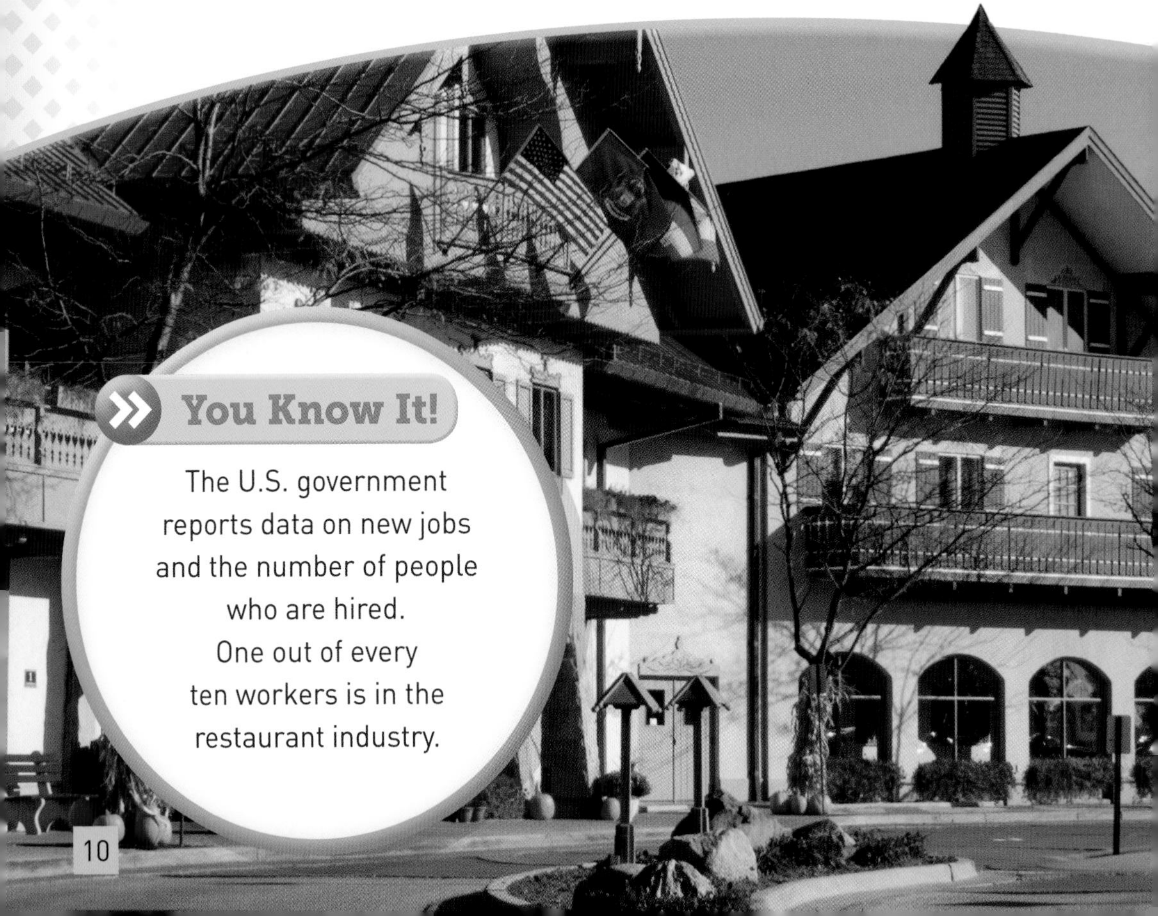

>> You Know It!

The U.S. government reports data on new jobs and the number of people who are hired. One out of every ten workers is in the restaurant industry.

"We have to do a lot of planning," she says. "We plan a year out. We plan a month out, and then, we plan a week out." She learned to make sales **projections** both on the job and in business school.

Path for a Manager

Can you see yourself keeping customers happy? What about training staff? Do you think you can make a business plan? Saying yes is the first step to becoming a manager.

Skills
Need communication, leadership, and STEM skills (to manage money and **data**)

Duties
Hire workers. Pay and manage staff. Make sales projections. Order food and supplies. Keep up with paperwork, such as making sure the **licenses** stay current.

Education
1. Earn an **associate's degree** or a **bachelor's degree** in restaurant management or **hospitality**.

2. Classes should include business and accounting, and adding a **master's degree** in business can help.

3. Be willing to work up from various roles in the field.

Marketing the Meals

"As a pizza, a disaster. As an Italian version of French onion soup, magnificent."
—from a real review of pizza at a restaurant in Texas

The top restaurants have to work hard to stay on top. A supplier might run out of ripe tomatoes. Or the best servers may call in sick. Each day a new set of problems pops up. Meanwhile the doors stay open. Customers are posting pictures of their meals online. They are sharing their thoughts about the food and service.

People often check restaurant reviews to find places to eat. Customers also look for places to avoid. So a bad night can hurt business. This is one reason why restaurants often have jobs for public relations (PR) people.

Image and Imagination

The PR workers' job is to keep their restaurants popular. They post facts about the food and special events. They form a **strategy** that encourages new people to visit and keeps regular customers happy. The PR workers need to communicate with people both inside and outside the business.

Some PR workers post food photos on social media web sites.

A typical day for a PR person at a fine restaurant may start with a meeting with the chef. The worker may taste new items on the menu, to know how to describe the meals.

At a chain restaurant's office, a marketing team may talk about ways to attract new customers. They may send text messages or emails with special offers. They may make special gift cards for loyal customers. These workers need STEM skills to figure out ways to raise the amount of money earned by the business. They need computer skills to keep track of everything.

Living Science

"If you want to become a great chef, you have to work with great chefs."
—*Gordon Ramsey, celebrity chef*

The chef runs the kitchen and sets the tone. He or she is the creative center of a fine dining restaurant. The other workers look to the chef for leadership.

"The chefs' passion for food and life is most obvious when they eat," says Matt Sadownick. He is a cook in New York City who trained at CIA (Culinary Institute of America).

>> **You Know It!**

In 1961, First Lady Jacqueline Kennedy was the first to hire an **executive chef** for the White House.

CIA is a **culinary** school in New York state. More people than ever are going to cooking schools, in part because of the fame that some chefs enjoy. But one of the school's directors has said that their best students are not trying to be famous. The best are focused on making great food for others to enjoy.

omelette shoppe

Be Our Guest

The place where Sadownick works as a line cook is popular and busy. "Everyone in the restaurant works hard to create a memorable experience," he says. "That is hospitality—the feeling when you eat something special or when you can give someone something special to eat."

In the culinary schools, future chefs study food preparation. They learn how to run a business. Then they get jobs in kitchens and work their way up. Some would-be chefs simply start at the bottom and learn on the job.

Where can chefs work besides restaurants?
Skilled cooks can work as personal chefs for people who pay to have someone run their kitchens. Great cooks can also become **corporate chefs**. For example, a chain may have a test kitchen, where chefs prepare new items. Hospitals, theme parks, cruise ships, hotels, and casinos all have chefs as well.

In the Kitchen

The kitchen workers often stand at long tables. They must pay attention to what they are doing. So to move hot pots they call out, "Behind you!" Sometimes an assistant is responsible for carrying things and calling out the cues. There is no time to waste. In a busy kitchen the movement of the workers becomes a kind of dance.

Chefs often start as chef assistants. These helpers clean tools. Or they may order supplies. Assistants may also prepare some foods. For example, they might chop vegetables.

» You Know It!

Most top chefs train an average of 21 years to get to the top position, according to a recent survey by a magazine for chefs.

Kitchens Little and Big

Sous chef (SOO-chef) means "under chef" in French. He or she is second in command. There may also be a kitchen manager. Some of the other usual jobs in a large kitchen include the following:

- Station chef, in charge of one area of the kitchen, such as roasted foods
- Pantry chef, one of the station chefs, in charge of cold foods
- Roundsman, replaces station chefs as needed

17

Focus and Teamwork

The line cooks pass plates along, and they add what is needed. There are cold stations where things like salads get produced. At hot stations the warm food is put together. Someone may work with sauces. Someone else may work with soups. It usually requires more safety skills to work at a hot station.

>> You Know It!

World's smallest: There are three places in Europe with just one table. Each battles for the title of smallest restaurant in the world. **Largest in the world:** There is one restaurant in Damascus, Syria that has more than 6,000 seats! (as of 2015)

Young cooks need to be able to take instruction. "Every young cook must understand how important the relationship to each person and piece of equipment is," says Sadownick. "Everyone needs a clean station and a clear mind."

Visions of Success

Some cooks started out as dishwashers. Another first job is that of porter. In some places, porters are called in at the end of the night to help with the cleaning.

Guy Fieri is a chef who owns restaurants. He also appears on TV shows. But his success did not just happen. Fieri has been working for this a long time. In the fourth grade he opened a business called Awesome Pretzel. Later, he washed dishes to save money for a trip to France to study French cooking.

Pop-Up Places

Sometimes a chef will serve new foods on a food truck or at a pop-up station. This is a way to get attention. By taking his or her best foods out into the public, a chef can find new fans. A food truck is a restaurant on wheels. It can be pulled up to a curb in a busy city, or it can be taken to events like fairs or farmers markets. A pop-up is a restaurant set inside a space, such as a park or warehouse, for a short time. It can appear and reappear in different spaces.

Talking to a Teaching Chef

Sue Slater works at Cabrillo College in Aptos, California. She is the head of the culinary program. Her students run a restaurant and produce special events, such as weddings. She has a degree in food service technology and a second degree in business. Slater earned diplomas from Le Cordon Bleu, in Paris, and the Academy of Wine, in Spain. Before becoming a full-time teacher, she worked as a line cook and a sous chef. She was the top chef and owner of a catering business.

1 What happens at the culinary school?

We have degrees in culinary arts and hospitality management. We offer skills **certificates** in baking, cooking, catering, and wine skills. We have lectures and labs. It's a two-part education. We've got a very complete program at the school.

We have a catering lab now. You know, we do weddings here during the summer. We have a wedding with 150 guests tomorrow. It's serious stuff, and the students do it all.

2 **What was your first step toward becoming a chef?**

I would tear out recipes. I started a notebook of recipes and began experimenting at an early age.

3 **What would you tell a student who wants to become a chef?**

Play with your food. Keep cooking, and most of all experiment. Remember, a recipe is just a guideline.

And you've got to know, you are going to fail sometimes. But you learn from your failures.

Front of the House

"It costs a company more to get new customers than to keep the ones it has."
—Denise Lee Yohn, restaurant marketing expert

Greeters and hosts work up front. So do the servers and the people who take dirty plates away. Experts say the most important skills for these jobs are being friendly and organized. These workers need to think fast, too.

Many customers ask for their seats ahead of time. They make reservations. Other people just walk in and hope tables are open. The workers in front have to manage the flow. The trick is to make sure people with reservations do not wait. The regular customers need special attention so they will return often.

Please Be Seated

STEM skills can make a difference in this business. For example, an owner of a restaurant in Chicago studied data about his visitors. He kept thinking about it. He thought he could improve the flow by selling tickets for the seats.

It worked! Now his tickets cost more on busy nights. The place charges less when it's less busy. He has made a new computer program to go with his plan. Could this be the future for popular restaurants?

What different kinds of restaurants are there?

Full-serve restaurants seat diners, and the staff takes orders and delivers food to tables in the dining area.

Fine dining is full serve with specialty food or a formal dining room.

Casual dining may be full serve, but prices are usually low and there is less personal service.

Quick-serve places usually have counters where customers order food rather than tables and table servers.

Fast-casual places are part casual dining and part quick serve.

Front and Center

Fancy restaurants sometimes have a maître d' (MAY-trah-DEE). The name comes from a French saying that means "master of the house." This person is in charge of the servers. Sometimes, the same person will go to a table to prepare a fancy dish. Working in front is like being a performer in more ways than one.

Taking a Tip

Servers get tips. Customers who value the servers' work leave extra money to show that they are thankful. Often, the head of the servers, or the manager, divides the tips received at the end of the day.

Businesses where workers earn tips do not have to pay the minimum wage. That is the least amount of money per hour paid to someone by law. So, tips are important to the workers. Quite often all or some of the tips goes into a pool. The rest of the workers, such as those who clear the tables, share the extra money. The money earned from tips is important to workers in restaurants and **cafés**.

How much do people tip in the United States?

It is usual to tip 15 percent to 20 percent of the bill before taxes. When a group stays longer than normal on a busy night, the amount may be higher. The tip at a self-serve or quick-serve restaurant is often lower, maybe 10 to 15 percent if there is some sort of worker bringing food or drinks or clearing tables. Fast-food workers do not usually get tips.

Supporting Roles in Dining

Many kinds of workers have important roles in dining. You do not always see them. But they help to create an experience that customers will enjoy and remember. A great deal of care and preparation goes into each dish, especially at a fine dining restaurant.

Accountant

It is the accountant's job to keep track of money that comes in and bills that get paid out. If the restaurant keeps good records, an accountant may need to show up only on occasion. Some owners do their own accounting.

Beverage Manager

This manager's job is to offer popular drinks and stock them. He or she makes sure everyone knows how and when to serve the drinks. This is especially important when a restaurant serves wine and other drinks with alcohol.

Expediter

This person works in the kitchen but does not cook. This role is needed in kitchens that are very busy. He or she might organize the orders, to help make sure everything comes out on time. This person may also place garnishes on the plates during very busy times.

Prep Cook

This worker does tasks that need to be done early in the day. For example, prep cooks chop vegetables for salads. They make frosting for cakes. The prep cooks are often in charge of food storage. So, they need to know what makes foods rot or taste odd during storage.

Science of Success

Cooking and baking are sciences. A chef knows that eggs will bind a cake together. The flour acts as the main structure. Baking powder and baking soda release a gas called carbon dioxide. This adds bubbles to the batter and air to the cake.

The restaurant business is a science as well. "Math is important to us," says Grossi, the general manager of the Bavarian Inn. "We look at a lot of numbers, and we make good **estimates**. From that our different teams have to take our numbers and make orders."

"We look at last year's numbers, how many meals were served, for example. And what average meals cost us and compare our costs to what we earn on an average meal. We follow food trends," she says. "We set objectives and goals."

At Work in Restaurants

General Manager. Executive Chef. Host. Food Scientist. Line Cook. Pastry Chef. Public Relations Manager. Accountant.

In a dining room, the customers eat and talk. They make memories. In the background are people with a wide host of skills. They have followed their interests to this important industry. In a restaurant they can use their skills to help others.

Do you like to make food and to think of new ways to serve it?

Does it please you to make people happy?

Can you see yourself putting in long hours and lots of effort to build a successful career?

Perhaps you will one day find yourself on the job . . . in a restaurant.

Extension
Four-Star Review!

Think about restaurants that you know about, and choose one to review. You may even consider taking photos with a camera phone if you get permission first.

Before

Do some background work. Take notes on facts you need to pass along, such as where the restaurant is located, when it is open, and the type of food it serves. If you cannot go to a restaurant, you can make one up. You can "review" an invented meal.

Look up reviews in newspapers or magazines. See which are the most interesting. Aim to use the same kind of language. Use the power of words that appeal to the senses.

During

Pay attention to the meal that you are eating. Is there a proper name for the dish that you order? Name it. Describe it. Explain how it tastes. Pay attention to the service, too.

After

Review your facts, and write a review. Give pros and cons. Include your thoughts about how the place was decorated and how it felt to sit there. (Was it comfortable? Did it feel crowded/loud?) All of these details are part of your experience.

When making a point, be sure to give a detail that supports your thought.

Glossary

associate's degree earned for one or two years of study after high school

bachelor's degree earned for three to five years of study after high school

cafés small restaurants serving lighter meals

cater to provide food and drink

certificates papers with statements that give proof of something

corporate chefs cooks who work for large chains or companies

culinary having to do with cooking

data facts and figures

degrees notices awarded to people for advanced study

economy wealth and resources of a place; production of goods and services

environment surroundings or conditions

estimates guesses as to the final cost or value of something

executive chef chief cook in a large kitchen

garnishes decorations for food

hospitality the business of entertaining visitors

inventory complete list of ingredients or stock on hand

licenses notices of permission to perform something

master's degree earned for mastery of subject at least one year beyond bachelor's degree

profession work that involves serving or helping others

projections forecasts or plans made after study

protein class of compounds needed by living things

retail having to do with sale of goods to the public

strategy plan of action

technology science applied to life and industry

Index

>> Meet the Author

Jessica Cohn has made a career of writing and editing materials for young people, covering varied topics, from social studies and science to poetry. If you ask her, Cohn will tell you that she feels lucky to be on the job in educational publishing. Each day, she discovers something new to learn and someone with an interesting story—and then gets to share the information. Jessica and her family reside in California. When not working, she enjoys hiking, helping her local library, and exploring the country.